SELF-APPROVED

Affirmations in Action

WEEKLY JOURNAL

This Journal Belongs to:

_____

Self-Approved; Affirmations in Action a 52-Week Affirmation Journal
Copyright © 2018 Necie Black

ISBN-13: 978-0-9984552-2-8

Self-Approved

Affirmations in Action

"This is all about the GIFT you are to the world.
You were born to be special and to contribute
something amazing. The gift you have inside must
be opened and shared. By the way, in case you're
wondering, your GIFT is what lights up your soul."
– Kim Coles

Affirmations __in__ Action is not your everyday journal. It is a 52-week recording of your thoughts and actions towards building an authentic and purpose filled life. Expect these pages to prompt you to consider what is working well and what isn't.

No judgment. No guilt. No defensiveness. Instead, this is a safe place for self-reflection and assessment.

The journal begins each week with an affirmation and an action, both requiring introspection. If an affirmation or action docsn't apply, write your own. Push past doubt or fear to gain more clarity for your life. Use every line and space, from the front cover to the back and record your beliefs, hopes and dreams.

It doesn't matter if today is your first day experiencing affirmations or you're a seasoned believer in them, you will explore something new about yourself. Stand in agreement *with* you about *you*. Give yourself permission to validate and approve everything unique and beautifully you. As your faith grows, so will the strength of your affirmation and the power you possess.

Necie

3

SELF-APPROVED
Affirmations in Action

WEEK 1 Affirmation:

"God is my creator and His love makes me worthy of all good things. God blesses and approves of me."

*Date*_____

Action:

Take a moment and reflect on the value of God's presence in your life. What is the hope of your faith and your relationship with him?

_____

_____

_____

_____

_____

_____

_____

_____

_____

_____

_____

_____

_____

_____

_____

_____

_____

_____

_____

_____

_____

_____

Create a Faith Affirmation:

Thoughts for the week:

SELF-APPROVED
Affirmations in Action

WEEK 2 Affirmation:

"I am happy, confident and finally clear about my worth. I am true to my best self."

Action:

*Most people believe the negative things others say about them. Were you conditioned to see yourself as anything but wonderful? Who do **you** say you are?*

_____

_____

_____

_____

_____

_____

_____

_____

_____

_____

_____

_____

_____

_____

_____

_____

_____

_____

_____

_____

Create a Self-Love Affirmation:

Thoughts for the week:

_____

_____

_____

_____

_____

_____

_____

_____

_____

_____

_____

_____

_____

_____

_____

_____

SELF-APPROVED
Affirmations in Action

WEEK 3 Affirmation:

"I commit to being great. I channel my authentic energy when sharing who I am with others."

Action:

What does authenticity mean to you? Share an example of an authentic moment, when you were your true self. How was this energy empowering?

_____

_____

_____

_____

_____

_____

_____

_____

_____

_____

_____

_____

_____

_____

_____

_____

_____

_____

_____

_____

_____

Create an Authenticity Affirmation:

Thoughts for the week:

_____

_____

_____

_____

_____

_____

_____

_____

_____

_____

_____

_____

_____

_____

_____

_____

_____

SELF-APPROVED
Affirmations in Action

WEEK 4 Affirmation:

"I have a beauty that shines from within. It allows me to be secure and true to my unique presence in the world."

Action:

Allow your inner beauty to speak for you. Write ten (10) things you love the most about who you are. You are amazing; admit it and repeat what you love about yourself every day.

_____

_____

_____

_____

_____

_____

_____

_____

_____

_____

_____

_____

_____

_____

_____

_____

_____

_____

_____

_____

Create a Beauty Affirmation:

Thoughts for the week:

SELF-APPROVED
Affirmations in Action

WEEK 5 Affirmation:

"My body is a temple and I treat it with dignity, love and respect at all times. I am comfortable with my shape, form and physical features."

_Date_____

Action:

Don't be shy. Bare it all in the mirror and take a good look at your body; you are unlike any other. What ten (10) physical features do you love most about you? How do they represent your authenticity?

_____

_____

_____

_____

_____

_____

_____

_____

_____

_____

_____

_____

_____

_____

_____

_____

_____

_____

_____

_____

Create a Body-Confidence Affirmation:

Thoughts for the week:

_____

_____

_____

_____

_____

_____

_____

_____

_____

_____

_____

_____

_____

_____

_____

_____

SELF-APPROVED
Affirmations in Action

WEEK 6 Affirmation:

"Self-care is a priority. I am diligent in taking time for myself, without feelings of guilt."

*Date*_____

Action:

With your demanding schedule, how do you put yourself first and make "me" time non-negotiable? What do you feel may be missing in your self-care and what will you do about it?

_____

_____

_____

_____

_____

_____

_____

_____

_____

_____

_____

_____

_____

_____

_____

_____

_____

_____

_____

_____

Create a Self-Care Affirmation

Thoughts for the week:

SELF-APPROVED
Affirmations in Action

WEEK 7 Affirmation

"I am thriving in a life filled with prosperity and abundance."

Action:

Close your eyes and imagine what it would be like to be prosperous. How does prosperity look and feel beyond where you are at the moment? Write it down. What impact can prosperity make for your future?

_____

_____

_____

_____

_____

_____

_____

_____

_____

_____

_____

_____

_____

_____

_____

_____

_____

_____

Create a Prosperity Affirmation

Thoughts for the week:

_____

_____

_____

_____

_____

_____

_____

_____

_____

_____

_____

_____

_____

_____

_____

_____

_____

SELF-APPROVED
Affirmations in Action

WEEK 8 Affirmation

"I am at peace with the past and open my heart to new people, opportunities and blessings."

*Date*_____

Action:

The past has no control over you. Search your heart for remnants of fear, anger, hurt or blame that may be hindering your progress. What <u>must</u> you face in order to heal and release? Will you face it?

_____

_____

_____

_____

_____

_____

_____

_____

_____

_____

_____

_____

_____

_____

_____

_____

_____

_____

Create a Healing Affirmation

Thoughts for the week:

_____

_____

_____

_____

_____

_____

_____

_____

_____

_____

_____

_____

_____

_____

_____

_____

SELF-APPROVED
Affirmations in Action

WEEK 9 Affirmation

"I am becoming the woman God designed me to be. I strive to align with His greater purpose for my life."

Action:

Let's say it's a year from now. How is the woman you are in your future different from the woman you are today? Think about what must change for you to become her.

_____

_____

_____

_____

_____

_____

_____

_____

_____

_____

_____

_____

_____

_____

_____

_____

_____

_____

_____

Create an Alignment Affirmation

Thoughts for the week:

SELF-APPROVED
Affirmations in Action

WEEK 10 Affirmation

"I possess the courage to stand in my truth. Every day, without apology, I unmask all that is beautiful about me."

Action:

Write your truth. Are there parts of yourself you keep hidden away for fear of being hurt or rejected? What is preventing you from trusting, loving, being, doing and living the life you desire and deserve?

_____

_____

_____

_____

_____

_____

_____

_____

_____

_____

_____

_____

_____

_____

_____

_____

_____

_____

_____

Create a Truth Affirmation

Thoughts for the week:

_____

_____

_____

_____

_____

_____

_____

_____

_____

_____

_____

_____

_____

_____

_____

_____

SELF-APPROVED
Affirmations in Action

WEEK 11 Affirmation

"I walk upright in confidence. My posture is aligned, my shoulders are straight and my head is held high."

*Date*_____

Action:

Reflect on a moment when you felt your most confident. What was happening? How can you have more moments like this, especially when you don't feel your best?

_____

_____

_____

_____

_____

_____

_____

_____

_____

_____

_____

_____

_____

_____

_____

_____

_____

_____

_____

_____

Create a Confidence Affirmation

Thoughts for the week:

_____

_____

_____

_____

_____

_____

_____

_____

_____

_____

_____

_____

_____

_____

_____

_____

_____

SELF-APPROVED
Affirmations in Action

WEEK 12 Affirmation

"The meditation of my heart is calm, my thoughts are peaceful and my emotions are managed effectively. All areas of my life harmonize for my greater good."

*Date*_____

Action:

You juggle many things. What are you devoting time and energy to that would be best served in another area? How will you restructure what you do so all areas of your life support each other?

_____

_____

_____

_____

_____

_____

_____

_____

_____

_____

_____

_____

_____

_____

_____

_____

_____

_____

_____

_____

Create a Harmony Affirmation

Thoughts for the week:

SELF-APPROVED
Affirmations in Action

WEEK 13 Affirmation

"I meditate on inspiring words to remain positive, happy and centered in love."

Action:

Write as many positive words as come to mind. Remember your happiest moments involving the first five words. What is happening? How can you have more moments like these?

_____

_____

_____

_____

_____

_____

_____

_____

_____

_____

_____

_____

_____

_____

_____

_____

_____

_____

Create a Happiness Affirmation

Thoughts for the week:

_____

_____

_____

_____

_____

_____

_____

_____

_____

_____

_____

_____

_____

_____

_____

_____

SELF-APPROVED
Affirmations in Action

WEEK 14 Affirmation

"I pray, meditate and receive the direction I need to align my life with clarity and purpose."

Action:

Envision your life 10 or 20 years from now. How does prayer anchor what you believe about yourself and the path you have chosen? How will you stay focused on your vision?

_____

_____

_____

_____

_____

_____

_____

_____

_____

_____

_____

_____

_____

_____

_____

_____

_____

_____

_____

_____

Create an Aligning Affirmation

Thoughts for the week:

_____

_____

_____

_____

_____

_____

_____

_____

_____

_____

_____

_____

_____

_____

_____

SELF-APPROVED
Affirmations in Action

WEEK 15 Affirmation

*"I pursue an ideal healthy state for my body
and make time for physical activity."*

Action:

What is your current physical condition? How would improving your fitness impact your quality of life? What would you be able to do if you had more energy, strength and resilience?

_____

_____

_____

_____

_____

_____

_____

_____

_____

_____

_____

_____

_____

_____

_____

_____

_____

_____

_____

_____

Create a Fitness Affirmation

Thoughts for the week:

_____
_____
_____
_____
_____
_____
_____
_____
_____
_____
_____
_____
_____
_____
_____
_____

SELF-APPROVED
Affirmations in Action

WEEK 16 Affirmation

"My muscles are flexible and I am fit, strong and resilient. I commit to an excellent long-term healthy lifestyle."

Action:

Imagine what a healthy and active lifestyle looks like. Write three (3) health goals you will achieve within the next 12 months. How will starting now support your better long-term health?

_____

_____

_____

_____

_____

_____

_____

_____

_____

_____

_____

_____

_____

_____

_____

_____

_____

_____

_____

_____

Create a Health Affirmation

Thoughts for the week:

_____

_____

_____

_____

_____

_____

_____

_____

_____

_____

_____

_____

_____

_____

_____

_____

_____

SELF-APPROVED
Affirmations in Action

WEEK 17 Affirmation

"I eat foods that are loving and kind to my body and include the nutrients to build strong bones and functioning organs."

Action:

Review your current eating habits. How does what you eat and drink make you feel at the end of the day? What will you change in your diet to benefit your 12-month health goals from Week 16?

_____

_____

_____

_____

_____

_____

_____

_____

_____

_____

_____

_____

_____

_____

_____

_____

_____

_____

_____

_____

Create an Eating Affirmation

Thoughts for the week:

_____

_____

_____

_____

_____

_____

_____

_____

_____

_____

_____

_____

_____

_____

_____

_____

_____

_____

71

SELF-APPROVED
Affirmations in Action

WEEK 18 Affirmation

"I increase my body's physical strength, stamina and agility with daily exercise."

Action:

If you are not where you want to be with exercise, what prevents you from being more active? A little exercise makes a big difference. How will you start and stay committed to being active?

_____

_____

_____

_____

_____

_____

_____

_____

_____

_____

_____

_____

_____

_____

_____

_____

_____

_____

_____

_____

Create an Exercise Affirmation

Thoughts for the week:

_____

_____

_____

_____

_____

_____

_____

_____

_____

_____

_____

_____

_____

_____

_____

_____

SELF-APPROVED
Affirmations in Action

WEEK 19 Affirmation

"I have plenty of energy and it feels good to see and feel the impact that combining a good diet and exercise makes for my body."

Action:

Imagine it's a year from now and you have achieved the health goals you created in week 16. How has your health improved from where you started? What did you do differently?

_____

_____

_____

_____

_____

_____

_____

_____

_____

_____

_____

_____

_____

_____

_____

_____

_____

_____

_____

Create a Health Goal Affirmation

Thoughts for the week:

_____

_____

_____

_____

_____

_____

_____

_____

_____

_____

_____

_____

_____

_____

_____

_____

_____

SELF-APPROVED
Affirmations in Action

WEEK 20 Affirmation

"I am blessed with a generous spirit. I gladly support others with what I have and I'm capable of giving at the level I desire."

Date_____

Action:

*Philanthropy means to give and support the
welfare of others. Why is giving important and
how does it feel to give generously? What goals for
giving have you developed for the year?*

_____

_____

_____

_____

_____

_____

_____

_____

_____

_____

_____

_____

_____

_____

_____

_____

_____

_____

_____

Create a Giving Affirmation

Thoughts for the week:

_____

_____

_____

_____

_____

_____

_____

_____

_____

_____

_____

_____

_____

_____

_____

SELF-APPROVED
Affirmations in Action

WEEK 21 Affirmation

"I am more than enough. All I need to live an extraordinary life is within me."

Action:

You have many gifts. Think about what you enjoy. What skills come naturally? What do people say you're great at doing? How will you cultivate and use these gifts to flourish?

_____

_____

_____

_____

_____

_____

_____

_____

_____

_____

_____

_____

_____

_____

_____

_____

_____

_____

_____

Create a Talent Affirmation

Thoughts for the week:

SELF-APPROVED
Affirmations in Action

WEEK 22 Affirmation

"I am a thought leader who is mentally sharp. I possess the ability to birth new, creative and exciting ideas."

Action:

Your thoughts are tied to what you believe you can or cannot accomplish. When giving birth to new ideas, what limiting beliefs show up to impede your progress? How will you counter them?

_____

_____

_____

_____

_____

_____

_____

_____

_____

_____

_____

_____

Create a Mindset Affirmation

Thoughts for the week:

SELF-APPROVED
Affirmations in Action

WEEK 23 Affirmation

*"I am equipped with the tools and strategies
I need to focus, execute and achieve the goals
I create."*

Action:

As you explore new ideas, what is the biggest and scariest goal on your radar? What difference will achieving this goal make for you? Where will you begin and what resources do you need?

_____

_____

_____

_____

_____

_____

_____

_____

_____

_____

_____

_____

_____

_____

_____

_____

_____

_____

_____

_____

Create a Goals Affirmation

Thoughts for the week:

_____

_____

_____

_____

_____

_____

_____

_____

_____

_____

_____

_____

_____

_____

_____

_____

SELF-APPROVED
Affirmations in Action

WEEK 24 Affirmation

*"I believe in research and development.
Investing in my dream is effortless."*

Date_____

Action:

Investment includes time, money and talent. What other resources can you consider when investing? How will you form a network of talented people to support you?

_____

_____

_____

_____

_____

_____

_____

_____

_____

_____

_____

_____

_____

_____

_____

_____

_____

_____

_____

_____

Create an Investment Affirmation

Thoughts for the week:

_____

_____

_____

_____

_____

_____

_____

_____

_____

_____

_____

_____

_____

_____

_____

_____

SELF-APPROVED
Affirmations in Action

WEEK 25 Affirmation

"I deserve financial abundance. It is my birthright to give <u>and</u> receive."

Action:

What were you conditioned to believe about money or financial gain? Does this belief affect your ability to ask for what you want with the expectation of receiving?

_____

_____

_____

_____

_____

_____

_____

_____

_____

_____

_____

Create a Financial Affirmation

Thoughts for the week:

SELF-APPROVED
Affirmations in Action

WEEK 26 Affirmation

"I possess the ability to create wealth and have money in the bank to meet all my financial obligations."

Action:

What are your thoughts and tendencies toward money? What behavior will you change to balance wealth, debt and spending as you continue to be a good steward over all you are blessed to attain?

_____

_____

_____

_____

_____

_____

_____

_____

_____

_____

_____

_____

_____

_____

_____

_____

_____

_____

_____

Create a Goal Affirmation

Thoughts for the week:

_____

_____

_____

_____

_____

_____

_____

_____

_____

_____

_____

_____

_____

_____

_____

SELF-APPROVED
Affirmations in Action

WEEK 27 Affirmation

"I gladly receive blessings from unexpected sources and use them to build a stable financial future."

Action:

How will you design your long-term financial success? List three (3) short-term goals to achieve within the next 12 months. How will they lay the foundation for your future financial stability?

_____

_____

_____

_____

_____

_____

_____

_____

_____

_____

_____

_____

_____

_____

_____

_____

_____

_____

_____

Create a Financial Affirmation

Thoughts for the week:

SELF-APPROVED
Affirmations in Action

WEEK 28 Affirmation

"*Money finds its shortest path to me and consistently flows to fill every need. The works of my hands bring wealth.*"

Action:

Imagine it is a year from today. Describe how your life is different as a result of reaching your financial goals. What changed? How will you keep focus and stay on track?

_____

_____

_____

_____

_____

_____

_____

_____

_____

_____

_____

_____

_____

_____

_____

_____

_____

_____

_____

_____

Create a Financial Affirmation

Thoughts for the week:

SELF-APPROVED
Affirmations in Action

WEEK 29 Affirmation

"I am delighted to share my gifts with others as I attract relationships built on mutual respect and support."

Action:

Having good partnerships is important when building your empire. What qualities will you look for in the people you collaborate with? How do these qualities match your own?

_____

_____

_____

_____

_____

_____

_____

_____

_____

_____

_____

_____

_____

_____

_____

_____

_____

_____

_____

_____

Create a Relationship Affirmation

Thoughts for the week:

SELF-APPROVED
Affirmations in Action

WEEK 30 Affirmation

"I bring excellence and integrity to personal and professional relationships and surround myself with like-minded individuals."

Action:

Reflect on your relationships at home or work.
What would you improve? How can you raise
awareness of the contributions of others and
increase interdependence?

_____

_____

_____

_____

_____

_____

_____

_____

Create a Relationship Affirmation

Thoughts for the week:

SELF-APPROVED
Affirmations in Action

WEEK 31 Affirmation

"I have an authentic personality and am transparent when sharing my thoughts and ideas with others."

Action:

Being authentic is more than speaking your mind, especially if it is to the peril of others. How will you use authenticity to usher in harmony and inspire others in your relationships to share honestly?

_____

_____

_____

_____

_____

_____

_____

_____

_____

_____

_____

_____

_____

_____

_____

_____

_____

_____

_____

_____

Create an Authenticity Affirmation

Thoughts for the week:

SELF-APPROVED
Affirmations in Action

WEEK 32 Affirmation

"I live in harmony with the people in my relationships. Everyone's needs are met, including my own."

Action:

Whether to be heard, acknowledged or to have autonomy, certain needs must be met for interdependent relationships to thrive. What are your needs? How will you know they are met?

_____

_____

_____

_____

_____

_____

_____

_____

_____

_____

_____

_____

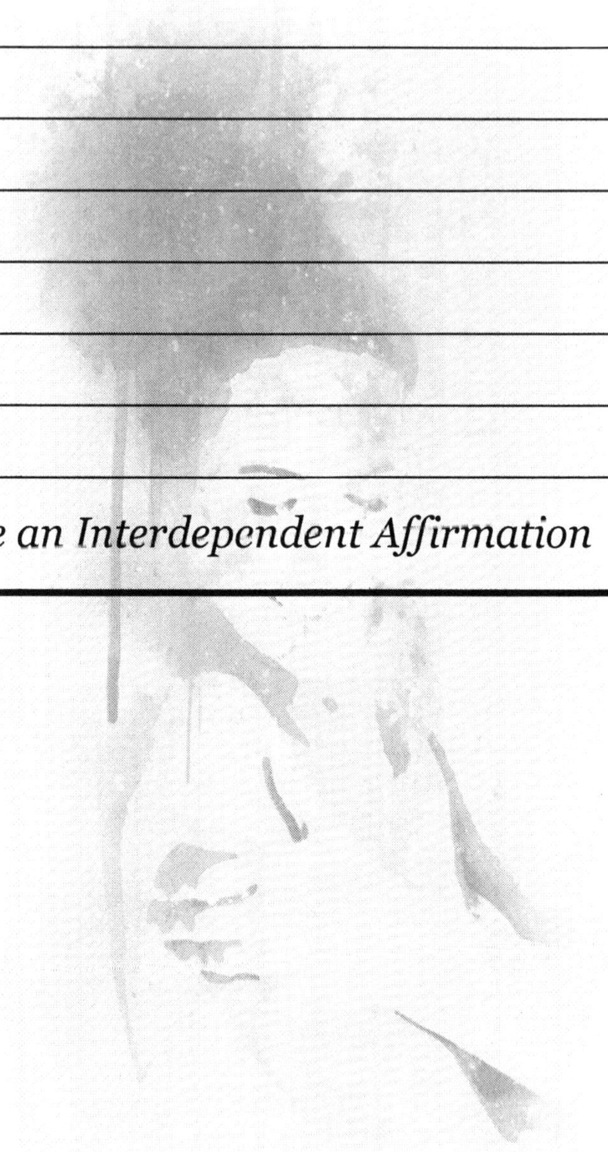

Create an Interdependent Affirmation

Thoughts for the week:

_____

_____

_____

_____

_____

_____

_____

_____

_____

_____

_____

_____

_____

_____

_____

_____

_____

_____

SELF-APPROVED
Affirmations in Action

WEEK 33 Affirmation

"I embrace diversity and my life is enriched with the unique differences others bring."

Action:

*How do you advocate an environment where
everyone's voice is honored, respected and heard?
What does providing such an environment say
about your courage and confidence?*

_____

_____

_____

_____

_____

_____

_____

_____

_____

_____

_____

_____

Create a Diversity Affirmation

Thoughts for the week:

SELF-APPROVED
Affirmations in Action

WEEK 34 Affirmation

"I nurture relationships where everyone brings their individual gifts and talents in support of our greater purpose."

*Date*_____

Action:

Imagine it's a year from today. How has your focus on interdependence affected the quality of your relationships? What did you do differently to create the change?

_____

_____

_____

_____

_____

_____

_____

_____

_____

_____

_____

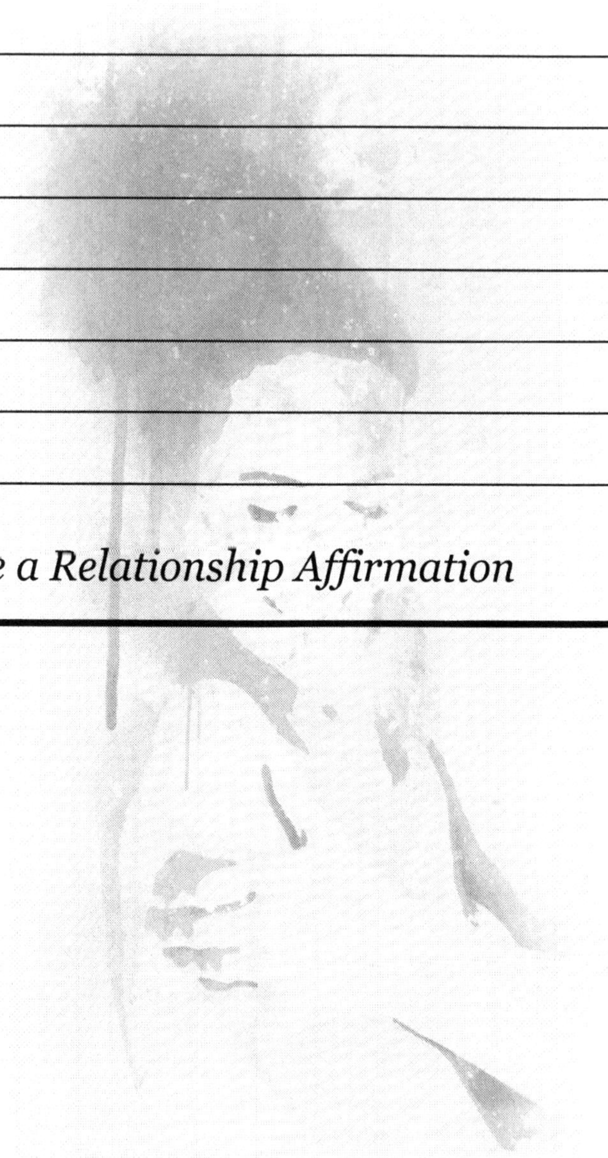

Create a Relationship Affirmation

Thoughts for the week:

SELF-APPROVED
Affirmations in Action

WEEK 35 Affirmation

"I love developing myself and exploring ideas to keep my senses engaged and my mind active."

Action:

Review your daily habits. Which activities support an active and engaged lifestyle? Which ones do not? What will you do to break unproductive habits and replace them with beneficial ones?

_____

_____

_____

_____

_____

_____

_____

_____

_____

_____

_____

_____

_____

_____

_____

_____

_____

_____

_____

Create a Healthy Habit Affirmation

Thoughts for the week:

SELF-APPROVED
Affirmations in Action

WEEK 36 Affirmation

"I am an overcomer. My will to live and persevere is stronger than I ever imagined."

Action:

Look at how far you've come and how much you have grown, in spite of adversity. What three (3) things are you especially proud of overcoming? How does it feel to have made it this far?

_____

_____

_____

_____

_____

_____

_____

_____

_____

_____

_____

_____

_____

_____

_____

_____

_____

_____

Create an Overcoming Affirmation

Thoughts for the week:

SELF-APPROVED
Affirmations in Action

WEEK 37 Affirmation

"*I am destined for great things. All obstacles are removed from my path.*"

*Date*_____

Action:

How do you feel about obstacles? What is your approach to getting through or around them? How does having obstacles build your character, strength and resolve?

_____

_____

_____

_____

_____

_____

_____

_____

_____

_____

_____

_____

_____

_____

_____

_____

_____

_____

_____

_____

Create a Strength Affirmation

Thoughts for the week:

_____

_____

_____

_____

_____

_____

_____

_____

_____

_____

_____

_____

_____

_____

_____

_____

SELF-APPROVED
Affirmations in Action

WEEK 38 Affirmation

"I am excited about what tomorrow will bring. Whatever I envision for my life manifests daily."

*Date*_____

Action:

What is your vision for life? Write 25 things you want to do, have or accomplish in the future, with no specific time constraints. Prioritize them in order of importance with #1 being the most important. What will you do with them?

_____

_____

_____

_____

_____

_____

_____

_____

_____

_____

_____

_____

_____

_____

_____

_____

_____

_____

_____

_____

Create a Vision Affirmation

Thoughts for the week:

_____

_____

_____

_____

_____

_____

_____

_____

_____

_____

_____

_____

_____

_____

SELF-APPROVED
Affirmations in Action

WEEK 39 Affirmation

"I open my heart and mind to reveal untapped potential and talent hidden away. I am developing new skills."

Action:

Think of how a new skillset will enhance your life, career, finances or relationships. What new thing do you want to learn? What are you curious about doing but have been afraid to try?

_____

_____

_____

_____

_____

_____

_____

_____

_____

_____

_____

_____

_____

_____

_____

_____

_____

_____

_____

Create an Exploration Affirmation

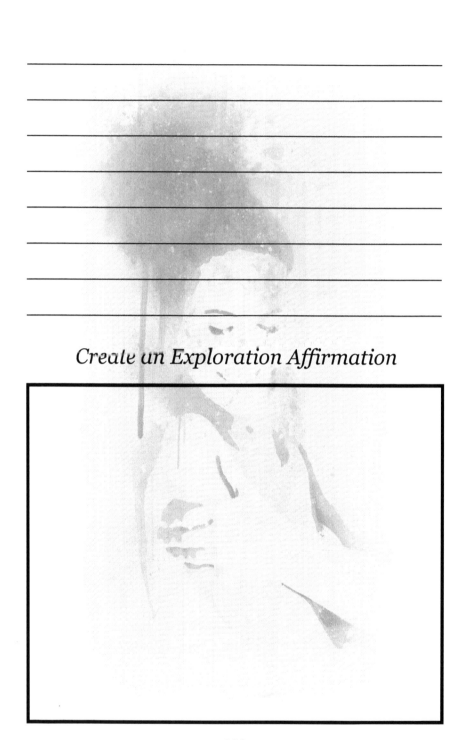

Thoughts for the week:

_____

_____

_____

_____

_____

_____

_____

_____

_____

_____

_____

_____

_____

_____

_____

SELF-APPROVED
Affirmations in Action

WEEK 40 Affirmation

"I am proactive in seeking every opportunity to expand my territory, increase the impact of my work and to grow in influence."

Action:

Do your own thing while you wait for other doors to open. What can you do to sharpen the skills you already have? How can you prepare for the new opportunities you seek?

_____

_____

_____

_____

_____

_____

_____

_____

_____

_____

_____

161

Create an Opportunity Affirmation

Thoughts for the week:

SELF-APPROVED
Affirmations in Action

WEEK 41 Affirmation

"I have a pioneering spirit and give myself permission to explore beyond where I am."

Date_____

Action:

Advancing into new territory can be scary. What fears might you hold about the unfamiliar? How will you move forward in spite of being afraid?

_____

_____

_____

_____

_____

_____

_____

_____

_____

_____

_____

_____

_____

_____

_____

_____

_____

_____

_____

_____

_____

Create a Pioneering Affirmation

Thoughts for the week:

SELF-APPROVED
Affirmations in Action

WEEK 42 Affirmation

"My grateful heart shows thanksgiving and humility as I seek to find the goodness in every person, place or thing."

Action:

A heart of gratitude produces a higher altitude.
Make a list of everything for which you are
grateful. What will you do to recognize and
celebrate the goodness every day brings?

_____

_____

_____

_____

_____

_____

_____

_____

_____

_____

_____

_____

_____

_____

_____

_____

_____

_____

Create a Gratitude Affirmation

Thoughts for the week:

SELF-APPROVED
Affirmations in Action

WEEK 43 Affirmation

"*Daily stress melts away because I give my mind and body the time it needs for sufficient rest and relaxation.*"

Action:

How does your body respond to different stages of stress? Write five (5) symptoms of stress you have experienced. What will you do to acknowledge, adjust and counter the effects of stress?

_____

_____

_____

_____

_____

_____

_____

_____

_____

_____

_____

_____

_____

_____

_____

_____

_____

_____

_____

Create a Stress-Less Affirmation

Thoughts for the week:

SELF-APPROVED
Affirmations in Action

WEEK 44 Affirmation

"I am worthy of love, respect and admiration. My presence provides an unprecedented amount of value to wherever I am."

Action:

Meditate on this statement: "My self-worth is based on who I am and not what I do. My value will never change." What are your thoughts?

_____

_____

_____

_____

_____

_____

_____

_____

_____

_____

_____

_____

_____

_____

_____

_____

_____

_____

_____

_____

Create a Self-Worth Affirmation

Thoughts for the week:

_____

_____

_____

_____

_____

_____

_____

_____

_____

_____

_____

_____

_____

_____

_____

_____

SELF-APPROVED
Affirmations in Action

WEEK 45 Affirmation

"I am a rare jewel and happy being me. There is no need to compare myself to anyone else."

Action:

How does it feel to watch others achieve success when you aren't progressing as quickly as you want? When you're unhappy with where you are, how can you resist comparing yourself to others?

_____

_____

_____

_____

_____

_____

_____

_____

_____

_____

_____

_____

_____

_____

_____

_____

_____

_____

_____

_____

Create a Self-Assured Affirmation

Thoughts for the week:

183

SELF-APPROVED
Affirmations in Action

WEEK 46 Affirmation

"Relationships are important for me and I focus only on light, love and a spirit of connecting."

Action:

Not all relationships work well. How do you decline the ones you believe are not good for you? What do you do when your needs aren't met in an existing relationship?

_____

_____

_____

_____

_____

_____

_____

_____

Create a Relationship Affirmation

Thoughts for the week:

_____

_____

_____

_____

_____

_____

_____

_____

_____

_____

_____

_____

_____

_____

_____

_____

_____

SELF-APPROVED
Affirmations in Action

WEEK 47 Affirmation

"I am blessed with the love and support of my amazing family and friends."

Action:

What works well in your relationships? What doesn't? What are three (3) goals you can achieve within the next 12 months for deeper satisfaction in your relationships?

_____

_____

_____

_____

_____

_____

_____

_____

_____

_____

_____

_____

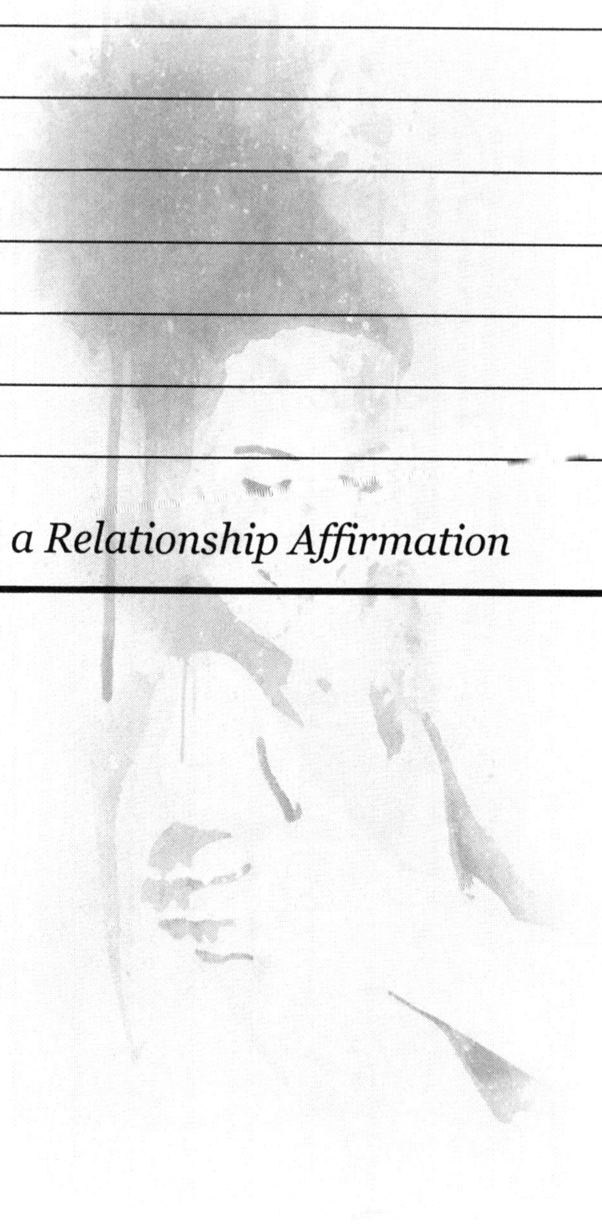

Create a Relationship Affirmation

Thoughts for the week:

_____

_____

_____

_____

_____

_____

_____

_____

_____

_____

_____

_____

_____

_____

_____

_____

_____

SELF-APPROVED
Affirmations in Action

WEEK 48 Affirmation

"I am full of joy and peace. People are attracted to my positive spirit."

Action:

Making a good impression is important when meeting people. Describe a moment where you met someone new. What positive statements did they make to confirm how you see yourself?

_____

_____

_____

_____

_____

_____

_____

_____

_____

_____

_____

_____

_____

_____

_____

_____

_____

_____

_____

Create a Joy Affirmation

Thoughts for the week:

SELF-APPROVED
Affirmations in Action

WEEK 49 Affirmation

"I am a sponge when it comes to gaining new skills and expertise. I enjoy learning and sharing information."

Action:

As you continue to network and connect, list five (5) skills you will learn by interacting with others. How will you share your knowledge and experiences with them?

_____

_____

_____

_____

_____

_____

_____

_____

_____

_____

_____

_____

_____

Create a Networking Affirmation

Thoughts for the week:

_____

_____

_____

_____

_____

_____

_____

_____

_____

_____

_____

_____

_____

_____

_____

_____

_____

SELF-APPROVED
Affirmations in Action

WEEK 50 Affirmation

"I am admired by others who see and appreciate me for who I am."

Action:

It's wonderful to be admired. How can resist becoming dependent on the praises of others? When no one applauds, how will you continue to celebrate who you are?

_____

_____

_____

_____

_____

_____

_____

_____

_____

_____

_____

_____

_____
_____
_____
_____
_____
_____
_____

Create a Self-Admiration Affirmation

Thoughts for the week:

_____

_____

_____

_____

_____

_____

_____

_____

_____

_____

_____

_____

_____

_____

_____

_____

SELF-APPROVED
Affirmations in Action

WEEK 51 Affirmation

"I am transparent in my words and deeds and encourage others to be comfortable expressing themselves."

Action:

What role do you believe transparency plays in communicating with others? How can you use transparency to improve the expression of your thoughts and ideas?

_____

_____

_____

_____

_____

_____

_____

_____

_____

_____

_____

_____

_____

_____

_____

_____

_____

_____

_____

Create a Transparency Affirmation

Thoughts for the week:

SELF-APPROVED
Affirmations in Action

WEEK 52 Affirmation

"I am an imperfect person and give myself and others grace over perfection in our daily walk with life."

Action:

Each day, as you strive to be, do and live your best, how will you calm the inner critic who insists on perfection? How will you allow grace instead?

_____

_____

_____

_____

_____

_____

_____

_____

_____

_____

_____

_____

_____

_____

_____

_____

_____

_____

_____

_____

_____

Create a Grace Affirmation

Thoughts for the week:

As an author, speaker and coach, Necie Black shares strategies for personal and professional growth. She helps clients see themselves clearly and utilize their strengths to build confidence and live an authentic lifestyle.

Confidence is something Necie is passionate about. After two failed marriages, she persevered through low self-esteem, regained her confidence and now helps others do the same. To honor her passion, she self-published and released *Self-Approved; A Guide for Authentic and Purposeful Living* in 2017.

Necie is a Strengths Strategy Certified Coach, Certified People Acuity Specialist™, a Master Lifestyle Coach and a 2018 member of Forbes Coaches Council. She holds a Master's in Business and serves her community as Board Development Chair with Dress for Success, Oklahoma City, a non-profit organization providing support, professional attire and tools to help women thrive in work and life. Necie lives in Oklahoma with her husband Michael.

Made in the USA
San Bernardino, CA
13 March 2018